Hedonism

Hedonism

Chris McCabe

Nine Arches Press

Hedonism
Chris McCabe

ISBN: 978-1-916760-26-4
eISBN: 978-1-916760-27-1

Copyright © Chris McCabe, 2025.

Cover collage © Chris McCabe, 2025.

All rights reserved. No part of this work may be reproduced, stored or transmitted in any form or by any means, graphic, electronic, recorded or mechanical, without the prior written permission of the publisher.

Chris McCabe has asserted his right under Section 77 of the Copyright, Designs and Patents Act 1988 to be identified as the author of this work.

First published September 2025 by:

Nine Arches Press
Studio 221, Zellig
Gibb Street, Deritend
Birmingham
B9 4AU
United Kingdom
www.ninearchespress.com

Printed in the United Kingdom on recycled paper by: Imprint Digital

Nine Arches Press is supported using public funding by Arts Council England.

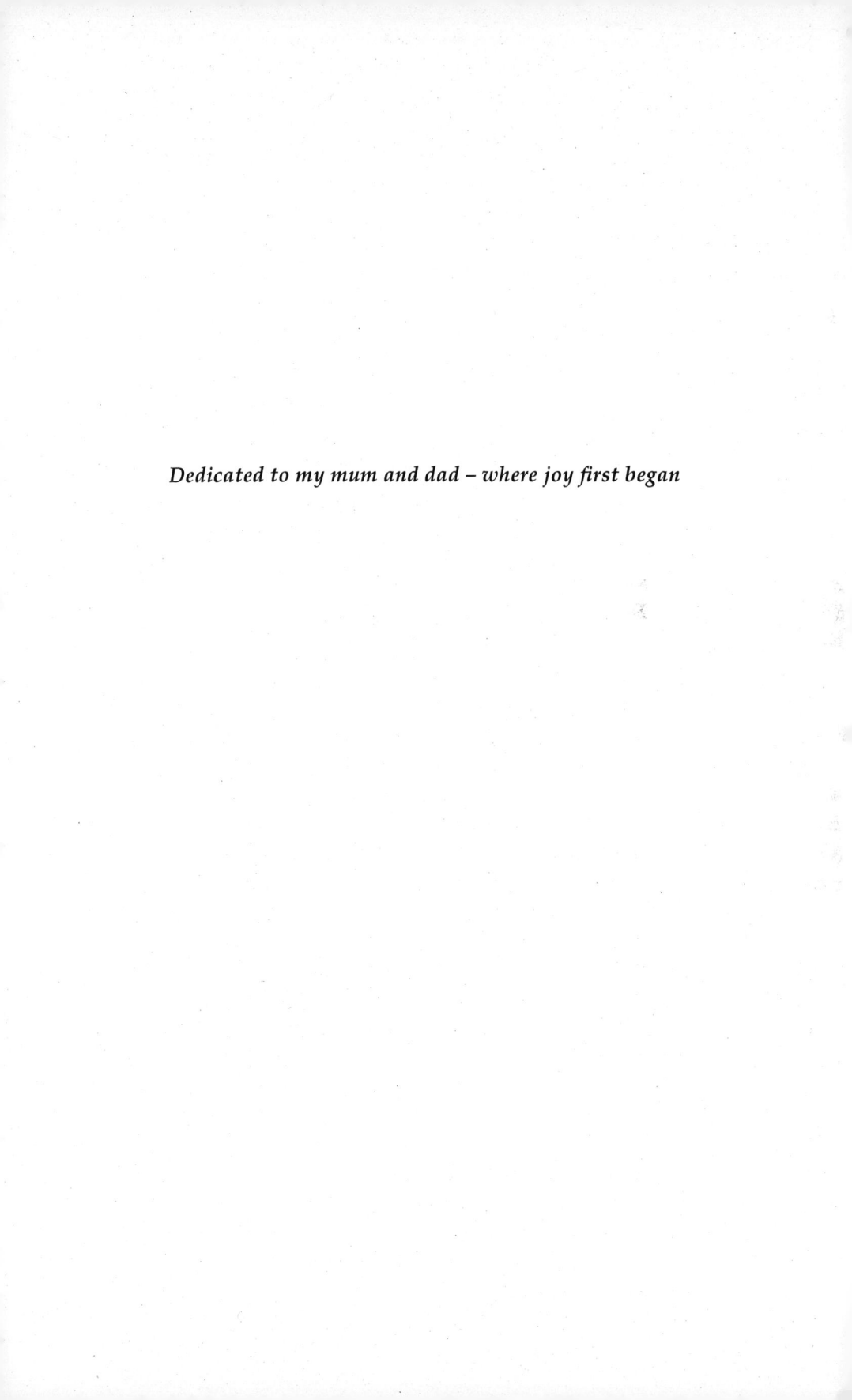

Dedicated to my mum and dad – where joy first began

Contents

Fathermade, Muttermatter	9
The Doppelgänger	12
The Machine	14
A poet & two translators	16
Ghosts at Sea	17
Meeting Mark Fisher	18
Cryptocurrencies	19
Poetry & Money	20
The Post-Brexit Poetry Festival	21
The Magus	22
A poet & two translators	23
Hippocampus	24
The Futurist Car Showroom	25
Brasília	26
For Kitchens	27
Scouse	29
Been living like this for days	30
LRB Lonely Hearts	32
A poet & two translators	33
The Rambling Boy of Pleasure	34
Threnody Of Radiation	35
Boss / the boss / dead boss	43
Then You Were	44
Shut Up Michael McClure	45
Lockedowne Aventure	46
Telemachus in Zante	49
The International Laughter Movement	50
A poet & two translators	51
Planes	52
For Kitchens	53
Jorge Luis Borges, Poultry Inspector	54

When the sun came to speak to me	55
Anschluss	56
How to speak Scouse	57
Then : A Ghost	58
A poet & two translators	59
Talk to that	60
Letter to Bez	61
Hypnotism	65
The Lord of Misrule	66
This Thing Happened	67
Hey	69
A Biography	70
Down on the Canal on Christmas Day	72
A poet & two translators	73
A walk through the Baltic	74
Notes	76
Acknowledgements	78

Fathermade, Muttermatter

Fathermade, mothermatter,
a seahorse hauled the ocean's load.
Mothermustered, fatherraider,
a lens scanned the sun's lost ode.
Pappamundi.

Motherust, fathersplatter,
a desert's negative exposed.
Fathershared, motherbloomer,
the body's shuttlecock de-rosed.
Mammapupa.

Fatherblustered, motherfeather,
the Turin Shroud was cloned.
Mothermad, Fathereacher,
our one sparse ship shed its node.
Patermapper.

after Gail McConnell

"Carnival is not a spectacle seen by the people; they live in it, and everyone participates… While carnival lasts, there is no other life outside it. During carnival time life is subject only to its laws, that is, the laws of its own freedom."

– **Mikhail Bakhtin**

The Doppelgänger

There's nothing more symmetrical
not even his interior. He sits facing
A man who is nothing but vapour
twins' the Doppelgänger thinks,
The Doppelgänger learns from the
measure himself for the eating.
says, 'like two vats of pasteurised milk
two priests fighting over the same Bible'.
be okay, but there is only one flood
one side for the light, the other for
through his corpus like a badly orientated
forged himself. When the Doppelgänger
space; when he dreams, he ricochets his
This is how it feels to have twice as much
The Doppelgänger looks through the
his organs glistening like a city of
'how about

than a Doppelgänger;
inwards like a haunted mirror.
has no cause to vape. 'My life has had
'and my thoughts the crew of the Medusa'.
snake, lies down next to himself to
'I sometimes feel I'm being watched', he
teaching each other how to sour'. 'Or like
If there were two Deuteronomies it might
& the Doppelgänger always fills twice :
the absorption of light. He has a waterline
banknote. Sometimes he worries he's
gets into bed, he tells himself to make
monsters from the amygdala to the cortex.
of everything & be half as full as anyone.
hospital glass, at himself under the knife,
glycerine. '*You're* doing okay', he says,
me?'

The Machine

Lying asleep walking
Last night I met my father
Who seemed pleased to see me.
He wanted to speak.
  – W.S. Graham

1

Dad, what are you doing with the machine?
You should have no need of it now you're dead.
This is my son you never met, connected
This side of rust. What force of dream
Allows the three of us to push a machine up a hill?
It's only to the base of the hill we need to go.
My brother goes ahead, ill-endowed with purpose,
As you stop us with a nerved hand, cubed with gold.
Why are we standing here, the three of us,
You fourteen years dead & my son still a boy?
Can you come back now? We've been waiting for you.
I told my son the story of you & the stale milk.
He's happy I think, but there's been a blank piece
For as long as you've been gone from this place.
It was Christmas Day when you climbed that tree
With a hipflask of vodka & a Holla to the wind.
What are we doing with this machine in any case?
As acid as sap the rust has ceased.
It's stranger than blood that you had to meet
Your grandson across the picket fence of sleep.
The three of us hold on to the machine.
It doesn't lose purchase on the slope.

2

Dad, where are you taking the machine now?
Is this death when you keep the machine for yourself?
You've made us redundant in this landscape, bleatfast with snow.
We watch you attach the machine to a motorway
And punch a first from the window as you speed into orbital.
The machine you've taken gave us such purpose.
What are we supposed to do now?
The keys are clenched in my son's tight fist.

A poet & two translators

A poet shouts at the stars; two translators open a window with a finger to their lips. And so, a partnership begins; the translators want to stretch themselves, the poet wants the world. 'Two translators are better than one', he thinks, 'just to be on the safe side.' When the poet begins to write prose the two translators call a meeting. 'This changes our contract', the first translator says, 'like you, we didn't get into this for money.' The poet puts a hand in the sharing nuts regardless of the many dactyls that have greased them. The translators bristle, like canvas tents from the 1960s. The second translator leans in, 'how many words are you thinking of writing?' 'Thinking of writing', the poet says, 'is like dreaming of sex or dancing with smoke.' After two more drinks the translators come around to the idea, 'will your prose be visionary, prompting us to invent a new bullseye in our target language?' The poet sighs. 'I'm writing the history of places that never existed. You might never see me again. I will send you a chapter each month, wrapped in calico. Ignore the postmark from Swindon.'

Ghosts at sea

Ghosts at sea specialise in eating other ghosts.
It's the way it is, just like business.
A career charting a life like a dreadnought
without a captain, steering itself like a magnet
through the Bering Strait of fifty years,
finding its outpost in photographs. Time to live?
But how do you practise what was only a shadow?
How do you dance on an island?
It's time to take a slow lunch outside a window,
watching the street, everything you didn't know.

Meeting Mark Fisher

'The slow cancellation of the future has been accompanied by a deflation of expectations'

– Mark Fisher

Sometimes I meet Mark Fisher down the pub. 'The good thing about hauntology', he says, 'is that no one really dies, they just live on, in a present which doesn't happen.' Fisher looks so normal, with his baggy jeans and Stooges T-shirt. Last time we met he recommended Japan Tricky Burial : all on the same evening. I spent the next three weeks typing text messages, *wtf Mark, this stuff is awesome!!!*, before realising I don't have his number. Instead, I write things down that I want to ask him next time we meet : *if culture is moving sideways will it fall off the edge? If we're haunted by unrealised futures do we live in a past of dreams?* The landlord accuses me of talking to myself. Yesterday someone told me Mark Fisher had died. It occurs to me he's been a ghost all along. Now it's only a matter of time until we meet for real.

Cryptocurrencies

O Love – for wanton cryptocurrencies I paved our way,
mining a million transactions like a tinker playing soldiers
with invisible lead. What seemed so real at first, dispersed –
leaving balls of dead bullion across our bed.

We mined & mined in dim unrealisation of our roles.
Told we were investing our power to unlock rare jewels,
we were but clerks, validating the status of a currency
that would not exist without the graft of lovers like us.

When we tried to cash it in
                              How fake are the stars?

Poetry & Money

Marx described Milton as a silkworm producing his work like silk,
outside of the marketplace. O sad Protestants,
who will inform the bees the Queen is dead,
before they atomise in berserk grammar? The swans meanwhile
are sailing towards Richmond, none the wiser, minting coins
of white bread to plug the intestines that don't belong to them.
Swans are nature's franking machines & they're never trialled
for insurrection. The Queen impersonator has given up,
out of respect, the way a shadow disappears in the midday sun.
The new king has been working for years to reduce his demands
on the public purse, not thinking that he could do this in a second,
through becoming, like Milton, a poet.

The Post-Brexit Poetry Festival

It's the Finn's fourth day of soup & his skin is glistening. His card
    reads : *Saint of Perpetual Silence.*
The Belgian is the Saint of Diplomatic Pralines. She's on an eternal quest
    for desserts that never come.
The Slovak is the Saint of Better Times; she talks of her happy childhood
    under communism & the cod surveillance of Covid.
She orders for the vegans as the chef racks up camemberts like UFOs
    in Area 51.
The German explains that there is no performance, only a disembodied
    voice in text. He is the Saint of Hauntology.
The Spaniard – the Saint of Shipshifters – speaks. 'Tonight', he says,
    'I'm going to cut so many new shapes
from the language there won't be any dough left on the planet.'
The Amsterdamer sighs, no one will believe her when she says the truth
    of the human voice is to be the DNA of the soul.
She is the Saint of Unrealised Possibilities.
The Croat is the Saint of Future Happenings. He's handwriting flyers
    for all the poets who are yet to visit his festival.
'Easy now', the Serb says, slicing into the white smelt of the cheese :
    'let's get through this first.'
The French poet agrees, looking towards the translators who are hunched
    over a desk. 'Is this the Nuremberg trials?' the American asks.
The English poet dusts down his suit, refusing to speak.

At the festival's final dinner the Finn has taped up his mouth.
The Slovak carries a dumpling on a piece of string.
The Belgian rubs at a chocolate moustache.
The German offers a rosary to his shadow.
The Spaniard is making an artwork from ring donuts.
The Serb & the Croat are standing each other shots.
The Hungarian has taped two dogs together, in the position they made famous.
The French poet has a finger on the elevator, hoping to leave the ground.
The American is smiling as the waiter brings the soups.
The Saint of Unrealised Possibilities has fallen asleep.
'Now', says the English poet, 'let me tell you what I'm Saint of.'

The Magus

The Magus spills green tea on the stars & asks why I'm wearing green.
'What shade is that for a dancer' he says, 'why not try some of this?'
He offers a block of Kildare sky but it's too bitter & my eyes are already blue.
The Magus is very much alive in the sense he still lives.
I was taught the alphabet was a magic slate, not this slightly manic Alpha male.
In Liverpool, a hundred kilos of fireworks are dispensed in Autumn so Winter
    lands like a blow-up dreadnought.
I thought the jack-in-the-box had gone berserk; O it was just my misaligned heart.
Too much minimalism is so heavy, I'm going maximal for my Tokyo years.
There's an amount of alcohol that burns your heart & an amount that warms
    your brain.
'Which do you want?' the Magus asks. Wafer-thin ham is the eucharist of
    the working class
and I should know : I was poll-taxed. Sea cadets are basically scouts with guns,
I failed a medical & became a medic. O Medici of Anfield, speak to your own.
The Magus clips his nails & calls them sickle. Time is honey & money the hive.

A poet & two translators

At a funeral, the poet & two translators take seats down an aisle; the first translator asks the poet to describe his grief. 'It's sharp', he says, 'like a flake of The Shard.' The translator writes 'he feels like shit' & shows it to the second translator. A priest appears & starts the engine on the service; it jolts for an hour & nobody gets up to push it. At the wake, the second translator checks-in on the poet. 'My despair is total', the poet says, 'like an unidentified pit, conducted for government experiment, on the fringes of Norfolk.' The translators compare notes over a flimsy plate of heavy pastries. 'He's sad, like darkness', the first translator says; 'what have you got?' The second translator covertly opens her notebook, showing two words in red ink : 'HE'S FAKING'.

Hippocampus

Hippocampus, region of the brain that is associated primarily with memory. The name hippocampus is derived from the Greek hippokampus (hippos, meaning "horse," and kampos, meaning "sea monster"), since the structure's shape resembles that of a seahorse.
   – Britannica

There's a seahorse in my brain, kissing my memories.
Neuronic silkworm, knitting memory from short-term algae.
Silkhorse printing vowels with its tail, beastworm of plasticity.
There should be a hippo in the cumulus, bumping the canoes of daydreams.
Wormhorse with a sardine's tail, salamander of synapses,
tell my mother there's something wrong with my amygdala, I'm furious
with good news, butting at sensation's fences – making the turnips gurn at the farmer.
Sea-ram, grow dorsals & glide with an alphabet known to the alligator.
Silkhorn, how soon is nostalgia? Print me. Skeptics call it blundered,
redundant, dirty & detritus. I call it mine & it thinks me with it.
Shrunken bunny, making interviews of my loneliness,
stimuli is a wild card in the forest of persistence, fishing my head
with an invisible rod; some call this poetry but seaworm calls it land.
Tiny god, tasselled prawn, how do you store memories like my very own eucharist?
You are rich in everything yet to take place, my body the road that feeds you.

The Futurist Car Showroom

'Come on! Let's go!' Marinetti said. 'Come on, my lads, let's get out of here!'

Futurists are living ghosts, like the self-hauntedness of Tony Blair,
spectral / spectographic / sparkplugs of machinistic thought,
medievalists of a culture-to-come, cruising in a six-gear typewriter,
mistaking quick print for acceleration & accumulation for progress,
stalling at time's hedgerow.

I hate cars.
Which means I hate Fascists, their manifestos written under a cosmos of asterisks,
forming a squadron drill against an army of stars,
throwing a mic-drop at a symposium of stokers –
firing an ocean liner with the dictionaries of workers.
When the Futurists met their Other, they called for the ravens of motorcars.
There goes Marinetti, with his monoclad lads,
the spectrum he could not face haunting a wingmirror.
There he goes now.

Brasília

for Pascal O'Loughlin

Is this Brasília?
We have a futurist cathedral
(for Catholics)
and you have a Pilot Plan
to reverse that indictment
of Lowry's
and build a utopia on the Wirral.
That terrible city
Whose main street is the ocean
Lowry wrote,
and now you walk it thinking 'I love this',
planning a detective novel
set along Seabank Road
where what has gone missing
is discovered,
the answers to all the arrhythmic years
of illness & death
will be found on the banks of the river,
in friendship,
where the Mersey spits back at the sixties
asking : you want my sound?
Listen to me spit it.

For Kitchens

The kitchen is a debating chamber
Dreamt to the scale of Europe
Today I shook hands with a mosquito
The washing machine turns its mechanic eye
I thought the kitchen was an operating system
Cool & functional as a Mac
One day it stops
And we shift to the next version

The gold cat from China is still waving at the sun
The fruit bowl gets heavier & no two plums ever taste the same
The last English mushrooms shrink back in the pan
Like the life cycle of a toad in reverse
What will this kitchen think of us while we're away?
It will slow down like a thatched-over country lane
A homemade film from the eighties
A fly will orchestrate coordinates, jubilant in its moon landing

This might be our last nuclear winter
September raises its flag in the wings of butterflies
Long exposure in avenues of light
We leave the ghosts on the other side of the glass
Last night they helped themselves to everything
The egg timer, the spatula, the flour scales
Then whipped up soul cakes
And ate them with a shot of Domestos

Three Goddesses come into my kitchen every night
The first is the Mother of Avant-Garage
The next is the Mother of Dreampop
And the third arrives with an obsidian wing
Across her eyes
She is the Mother of Shoegazing
Some people hear a Boeing wing in the fridge
But that is the Music of the Mothers

The drip of the tap
The filter in the fishtank
The mulch in the u-bend
Is Berlin in the seventies
London in the Poetry Wars
Liverpool in a beatnik permafrost

Kitchens are connected at night by air traffic control
They pass through timezones as we sleep

Scouse

First our voiceboxes were removed to our noses,
the grey quilts of ice & storm over the Irish Sea
gave us colds, which stayed as the seasons changed,
our children copied the adenoidal tang of how we talked,
then their children, then theirs, it was our homage to the Irish,
who gave us this, landing starved in our port to keep our pubs open
and women satisfied, which is to mean in laughter;
we fought like the Norse in a fang of redness,
fought with our voices that no longer sounded Lancashire,
that no longer sounded English, when pushed to it –
we were one third Irish, one third Welsh and one third phlegm,
We spat out this thing which made us stand out,
which separated us from them, we called it Scouse.

Been living like this for days

same thoughts
same things
been prowling these floors
looking for a loophole
been raging in my mind
and stuck behind glass
precise, like a cicada
dehydrating in prayer
been seeing my son
become trapped in his loops
like a circus artist
practicing art in view of his critics
he's on the same wire
but hasn't learned to fall
been learning how to watch
without knowing what to say
seeing the extra minute of sunlight
make tracks across the floor
each evening
gaining a centimetre more each day
been thinking of the past
how we have all lived like beatniks, now
even the mistakes earn their ticks
been watching the outside world
as if it's a cover
been waiting for it to change
for the hours to start to race
like untrained horses
through the streets
been learning new words
each day
wondering when I'll use them

been trying to read
been trying to listen
even tried to write something down
stepped into the shadow-song of a blackbird
met my mum in the park
walked through the graveyard
been around this way before
and know I could fall
and know I could pull through
watching my dreams
instead of the news
for some kind of prophecy

been wondering who we'll be
when this is over

LRB Lonely Hearts

Witty. Bilingual. Bibliophile.
The *LRB* ads (Lonely Hearts)
were too late for us,
faced (two faces)
up to the ceiling,
on the compactus
of a single bed.
I was reading *Nightwood*,
you gave me Irvine Welsh.

If I wrote /
And you read it /
Would you have replied /
You said.

A poet & two translators

The translators take the poet to play snooker. The first translator breaks, leaving the poet an easy red. It sinks like an eco-anxious view of the sun, presenting him a choice of colours. 'Blue' he nominates. 'Green nominated' says the first translator. 'I make it yellow' says the second. Both those colours are concealed by other balls. 'Blue' the poet repeats, adding : 'that would be an azure horizon on the first dawn of an old love newly lit by the perspective of age.' The second translator glares: 'aqua*marine* horizon'. The poet has accumulated a break of 55, the clearest sign of a misspent youth.

The Rambling Boy of Pleasure

for Niall McDevitt

The Rambling Boy of Pleasure takes the night bus, when the poets take the bucks,
knows a vision is more than sight, hears music in a craw,
gravitates where there is no gravity, 'cos to have no money is to levitate,
and what else is London for, but levitation, a gravitation to the place
speared by time, a mad whale chasing a wet man.
Theodore Roethke said every bat has a human face, but he hadn't visited
    One Canada Tower,
where every human has the face of a bat, don't ever touch flesh,
because the heart's sonar is a fire bell. So that's the bats,
but what about the elves, the gollums, the banshees, the cyclops & Balor?
London is a swamp for the mythic & out of it rises the Rambling Boy of Pleasure,
knowing capital is the root of evil, that bureaucrats pose as artists,
imbibing true songs behind the vellum of news, wearing their suits of blandest starch.
Remember that night, Rambling Boy, when you liquidated the Ancient Umbilical,
his ears of tin & Mephistopholes' grin,
because they were days our energies grew inside the Shipping News,
News from Nowhere & Housmans.
Nothing was subsidised, so much materialised
– the city darkens –
I see you walking next century, future exile, passing Blake on the Strand.
You always passed Blake on the Strand.

Threnody of Radiation

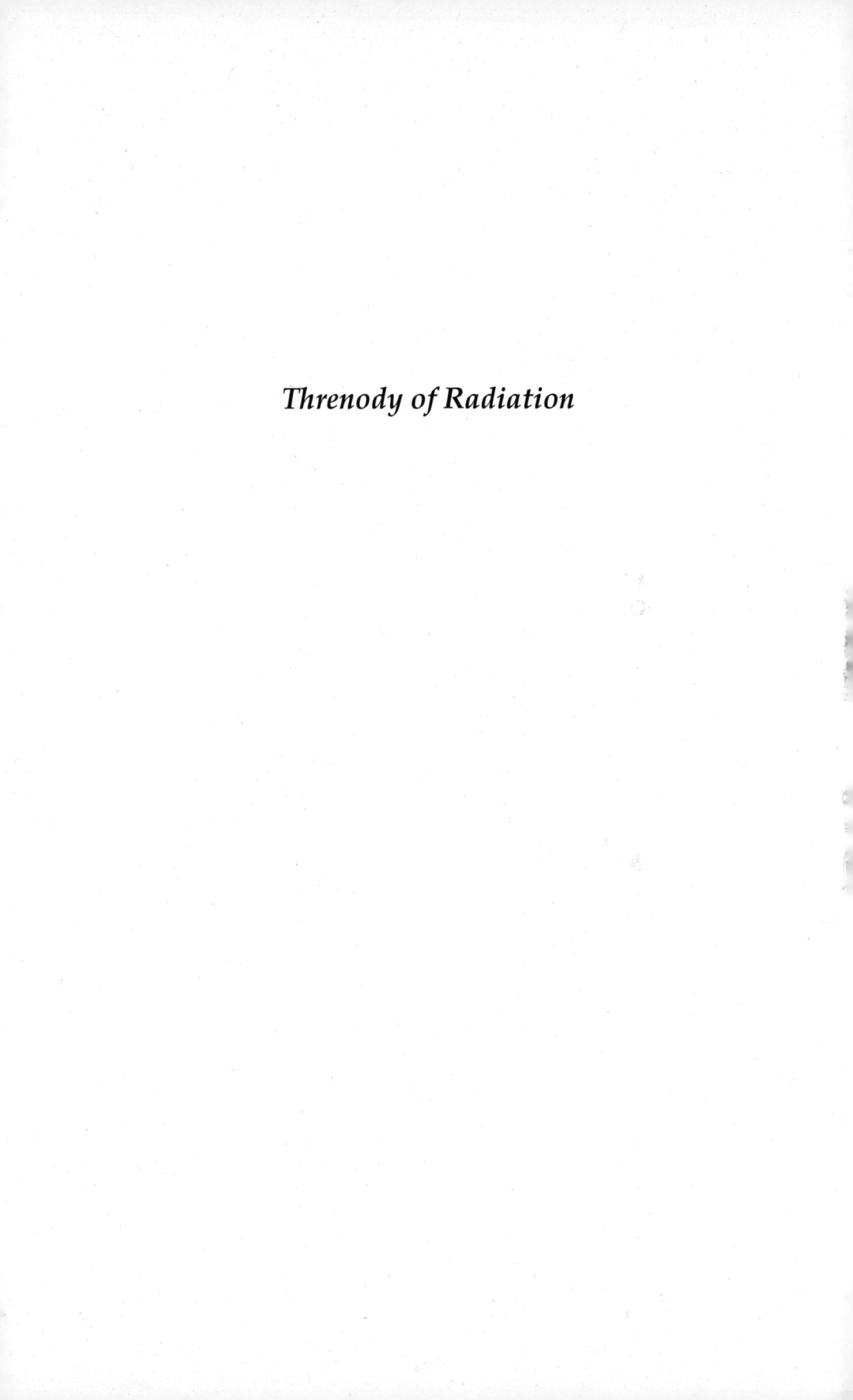

1

The land spills out its threnody, it won't deny it,
no fenland contains this river's source.
I dreamt distance into touch, your absence my hill,
I'd wake before the milkman's matins, to hitch a shadow
over fields & fish a lake.
In July the wind can sing a litany.
Nature wore a rind of motorway
and the kestrel fucked its invisible like a hare in a trap :
O God if I've willed you then just touch me.
I was ninety percent mud the rest of me wick,
the wick split in the mud so no one could light it.
My body was so much liquid I stared the lake into loam
watching the spectrograph of the damselfly
short-circuit the boatman's paradise,
as behind me those loping angels, the pylons,
willed us like priests into radiation.

2

When I was sixteen, I thought my coccyx was cancerous.
An exoskeleton rattled a solo appointment.
Since then I've tormented the doctor with lists :
the sunken hulk of depression
bass notes in my ears
anxiety sliding Aeolian scales.
Directors talk of 'The Span of Control', could I have some,
for the short-term immediate? Rolecreep
is a real thing & this is a fixed-term position I'm in
until the bellman & the hangman & the undertaker
& the ploughman meld to make a medley of my anachronisms.
We wasted those evenings on The Cut, in our twenties,
sharpened by The Strokes, cashing in our hand to spend
the night with ageing poets hunched under their bitterness.
What were we thinking? Their heart was in the highlands,
our minds on the mind of the other, what it was like to be touched,
to desire to think it like this or like that. Drink pulsed us together.
I swear I can hear the sea the song goes but I'm waiting
for some change, to hear it through the rain,
while the machine is stitching mechanical sutures
PLEASE SEEK ASSISTANCE
and there's no one in blue or orange to ask.
You're three hundred miles away & this bus is not in service.

3

In the clasp of the commuter rush
Through the cloister of the underground
I think of you in threnody of terror
Scanning the faces of thousands for a trace of fear
Crossy Road   Android poker   Emails on property
St Pancras foyers the free world of Europe
I hold the explosive of Robert Desnos
If this book was a brick it wouldn't make clearance
Desnos committed to the deep image
In trance states   Dreams   Under drink
Lover, if you suffer pain, never fear the river Seine
The station's forecourts & throughways
Cleansed silver-grey to highlight the ruffage of flesh
Tatty & textured   Clutching this brick
Which digital translates to a safe equation

The train leaves the restored carcass of Kings X
The poor in its ribs   surveillance makes them gnats
In its ecosystem
Pylons rig the marshlands
Glistering cars cloned for the sales yard
Containers cruising a high-rise bridge
The paradox of Ebbsfleet International
No one seeks glory in trans-capital terror
I think of you clearly   Your face
Amber eyes of *Yes*
This train pulsing to Ashford
I open the pages of Desnos –
Meet me today at Montparnasse

4

Not so much crow's feet as a kind of anemone
Calcifying the under-eyes   They've grown in just weeks
Sleepless nights & hours of talking
One night over Christmas
A strange sea-state ruptured from a dream
I saw you clearly & lost my balance
I've kept so much hidden from myself for years
There's nothing lost in facing this
This threnody of radiation
Your flight's in an hour   Your fingers in a rosary
I'm halfway there
I'll get off at the Seine   A bar
A walk along the river
An hour together in a hotel room
France no different through glass than England is
The skin around my eyes reflects in coils & vines
Like fingerprints
You made me see with

5

What's a passport anyway but a corrupted bible
A cloned work of apocrypha
Sold back to us by officials who lost touch with lyric?
I transport this tulip-bound edition
From my pocket to my bag
In a bar on Boulevard Montparnasse
On the screen Boy George emerges from a swimming pool
The bar staff swap high-fives
Your train from Charles de Gaulle is arriving soon

6

You make me question form again
What it is & why we need it
Your body curved by sea-spume
Your body I know better than my own
You read your poems near the Boulevard Montparnasse
The interviewer asks about form in your practice
'Urban buildings' you say
'Those who lived in them will recognise it'
And the music scores you learned to read at twelve
We pass through the avenue of the urban dead
Kiss at the tomb of Robert Desnos
A roped buoy floats on the granite
You descend into the mass
The only face in a station of the Metro
Still descending
Your outline   & symmetry
You turn & blow me back a kiss
Until tonight
The station transforms all you are
Into airspace

7

The snow blanks out all the days it couldn't be
Links snowfall to snowfall   Blake was right
All time takes place at once
My hand on your waist as a teenager
Our son on urban concrete shaping a snowform
The house at night knows that snow is there
Builds like silence around a pause
The snow falls as we conjure Robert Desnos
His body alive in a dead lover
What is my body doing here   packing a bag
Checking a ticket to London
Feet printing out steps
Marking an EXIT that is writ without me
Whose policy decrees we part today?
I'm wearing all black because snow is wasted
Without its opposite
There is no hearse
No mourning   Only steps
That accumulate like black cumulus
Only to evaporate

It isn't snow we leave behind
But its absence   the missing days

* * *

Boss / the boss / dead boss

def. *Boss;* Scouse dialect for something that is very good

It's all dead boss, boss-like; the Bossman
who owns all the power in the realm I detest,
but what most people forget is that power
serves up pleasure, discourse, & a texture that
the skint can't live without. So I called
to lay this out clear as day like : you are
the power I hate & can't live without.
So boss, King Bossa Nova, bossy bastard
of the winkplace, the first time I applied
for a job I forgot to add my return address.
Some mole-manager on the shopfloor opened
the seal, blinked, laughed, pinned it
to the noticeboard. What might've happened
if I'd have landed in the shelf-world of Huyton?
Would I have become a ledge? Farewell
aspirations for miniscule wage, Hello salary
that goes on calming the nerves it takes
to earn it. That's all we'd say : boss, dead boss,
boss the way this, & boss the way that.
When did I stop talking in the knotty-rings
of my adolescence? Can it be traced like a vein
to the waxed heart of advancement?
I stopped saying 'boss' when I became one.
What was it I forget I wanted to be?

Goodbye fuckin' boss world I set out to see.

Then you were

Then you were the bedroom & I was a seahorse
No waves without thought
You were the apple & I was the hoarding
No news but your scent
You were the hallway & I was the gardener
Gulls in our crow's nest
You were the bookcase & I was the basket
Such news ran through the shore
You were the yard & I was the attic
Our names forever in the steam
You were the kitchen & I was the cart
Would you go back there?
You were the undersheet & I was a stove
Nothing blue could pass our lips
You were the window & I was a boxing glove
No destiny without a map
You were the Ouija & I was a greenfinch

Who was the ghost?

Shut Up Michael McClure

No poet however Beat should roar their poetry to a cage of lions,
stand back Michael McClure, you're baiting an endangered species.
Poetry isn't a meat rack, but your body is fish carpaccio
garnished with a college sweater,
this isn't the way to take care of the language Mr McClure.
The Belarusian and Maori poets are in my cab
and there are ten red ravens circling over Fleet Street;
when we arrive at the glass building
the Belarusian says, 'the original must be faithful to the translation',
the Maori describes English as a Hydra.
Later
I buy a drink in the Hole in the Wall
while a Pole has an argument on his phone,
another cab arrives,
the Navajo Nation Poet Laureate tells how poetry came into her life,
O the Joy Harjo of its possibilities.
Laura Tohe, you make poetry because the Navajo need you,
Valzhyna Mort, you make language a future train with a diamond consignment,
I have heard poetry as an act of defiance,
I have heard poetry is the DNA of the poet,
I have heard poetry is brought by a raven,
I have even seen poetry dropped from a helicopter
but I have never seen poetry roared to a cat.
Shut up Michael McClure, the lions want their meat.

Lockedowne Aventure

A pilgrimage to buy a PlayStation, written in an invented language of Scouse, German and Middle English

It was de hundert daye of lockedowne
und we hat to travailen a hundert mylen
from de Porte Citie of Livingpoole
to de Canale Towne of Manchooser.
Our grayle was clar : to fynden for my sonne
de new FlayStathion, digitale modelle
(myne sonne liken de downeloaden).
We risen like de zon itself
to taken de rayle & boarden with spirits gud.
Den de aventure beginnen to chayngen
as de trayne manager maken a God in voice
on de tannoy & explaynen dat de paysengers
travailen from de Tower Two of Livingpoole
to de Tower Three of Manchooser maken
themselves layable to criminal charges
for traversen de laytest virus restrainens.
Myne sonne & me looken across de tayble
und blush : doen de FlayStathion maken excuse?
Myne sonne looken into de picksely skye
of hith fone as I konkokten a long spielen
to saye as to de rayson for our travailen.
To our grayte releefe no manager maken to
ask us of our reasone und we arriven den
in Piccadillie as liken two parts to one peece.
Now for de Tram Wagon to de towne
of Altrincham und de staw naymed Argos.
De Tram Wagon was boozie with like-mynded
travailers to de grossen Retayle Park
in de aforesayde Altrincham.
Und der wat byrds above de Matalan
und de Carpet Warehouse, a crowde
of blak-tipped gulls liken dead saylors returned

to lead us ever onwoods to de Argos. We
wayte at de playce called de chekout
for de FlayStathion to worken as alchemy
from de ordained number to de material goods
of de thynge itself. Und lo!
Like a tabernacle of de holiest ranke a maiden
of de Argos appearen from de bak of de staw
with de FlayStathion, this holiest altar
that is myne sonne's to taken forth as his.
We standen und see it shyne like de star
as Argos Maidens und de shawpers staren at de box.
Then comen forward de Maiden of Airforts
und asken, 'how did you retrieven de FlayStathion
wen so menny failen?' Myne sonne explainen
de trycke in de Chrome browse, to claren de cache
und finden 'click & collect' & callen downe
from de grayten god Argos de FlayStathion.
'Where do you vaygrants liven', she asken, und
we reply we abiden in Livingpoole. Den she
forwernen, 'Do not returnen on de Tram Wagon
through Altrincham for de scallies
und poachers of Manchooser will maken
of de FlayStathion their owne. Instead, comen
in myne wagon und I driven you to de Airfort.'
Und in a flashen myne sonne und me are in
de wagon, forgetten de lawe of de sociale distancen,
haws power purren for to taken
us onwoods for de Airfort. But lo! De engine
keepen kutten out, und de Maiden starten
to Text into her fone und I maken to panicken,
thinken dat she arrangen for her husbande & men
to intervenen in our aventure und taken
de FlayStathion for their ownen. Mine mynde playen
dese tryckes of duress until soonen
we arriven at Manchooser Airfort.

Und it is lyken de bleak landscaype of Ballard
dis place that hath no playnen in de heaven
nor no passengere on de grownd.
We thanken heartilee de Maiden und walken
in to de whitelande of de Airfort for to fynden
de trayne to Livingpoole. It happene next dat
de trayne not departen for an houre so we
maken for de Spar to quellen de appetyte dat
growen like de beare for victuals. We maken
with de flapjack und pretzels und deepen ridge
snacken for de trayne. But lo!
Due to virus restrainens we be forbiddene to eat
on boarde, so we finden de bench for to snacken.
At last we boarden with de FlayStathion but
this is not de ende of de tayle, for now boarden
de Vocalmouth of De Fone
who pronouncen de entirety of his mynde
into de wagon from Manchooser to Livingpoole.
'I hope I maken to be sectioned', he pronouncen,
'in order to receiven de gift of free rente'.
Und so awn und so awn he goen, 'I need
to sorten out my lyfe & taken a bath'
und so awn, until myne sonne und me must texten
to each und explainen dat dis is de parten
of de non-Lockedowne dat we missen not. Und all de whyle
de FlayStathion lyen between uns, it mynden not
de wynde talken by de Vocalmouth,
for like de God, it looken only forwarden,
as if for to unlocken its owne dreamen.

Telemachus in Zante
for Pavel

The snorkel turns his face to chrysalis.
He pushes a lifeboat from the coast.

At 11 he walks those two '1's
like rickety stilts into a granular sand.

His tan is half-done, like a shelled shrimp
yet to be turned on a grill.

He shouts facts to the balcony : *only female
mosquitoes bite; eggs incubate at the water's edge.*

One moment he clings, the next is torque-flash –
like a marlin out to joust the world's lens.

My Telemachus, unmoored Odysseus,
tell your father what the future is.

The International Laughter Movement

Touching down in Manchester the German flight attendant
is trying to make an announcement but corpses into the mic :
PLEASE KEEP YOUR SEATBE...
laughter burbles in her voice, gargles in her larynx,
until she can only split particles of accented English.
What's going on up there?
Like wildfire, laughter spreads through the plane,
lone-flyers are creased-up in their seats, breathing in
this invisible force, going viral through their bodies.
It blooms in shoulders, blossoms lungs, reddens faces ...
This is an international movement!
A new form, latching us to its flight path, to this air hostess
we can't see, who's still corpsing, negotiating the syntactical
with the breath, trying to parole logic while a monkey
clangs its symbolisms :
WILL FLIGHT CREW PLEA...
She bails again, bites nut-and bolt words into the jelly of paroxsyms,
losing at this war of communicating something she's bound by law to tell us,
    but it's too late for her now,
she's floating on the clouds mountains landscapes of laughter,
filling the plane with its illicit usefulness.

A poet & two translators

At Passport Control the poet & two translators hit a language barrier. 'Wohin fährst du?' the security official asks. The poet looks to the translators for guidance. 'She's asking if you've just passed wind' the first translator says. 'Ignore him', the second advises, 'she wants to know if you're a male witch.' The poet addresses the security official directly: 'Anything you can smell around me is the accumulation of a life of forensic exploration; I've lived equally amongst the grubs & the stars. I *am* a male witch, which is not the same thing as a wizard because, like Jung, I give my anima free expression in ways that a pointed hat would make light of. To pass through this gate negates the animal in my corpus that is led by light & intuition; what lies on the other side is what is required to feed my curiosity, which your system of barriers ridicules, like a clown burnt at the stake, melting in a shit-heap of plastic paints & synthetic onesies.' 'Ein Witz!' the guard laughs. The poet turns to the translators. Eyeliner is running down the first translator's cheeks, past the red ball at the end of her nose.

Planes

Named as they are for the Ikea-white of Swiss Air.
Icarus erected a bookcase, Daedalus deconstructed it.
The man in security says there's something in my bag,
I know what it is, no don't touch – I'll get it.
Mobile phones must now be stowed away,
inform the cabin crew if the device starts to smoke.
My love, at 5 a.m. in the dark of another city, I kissed
you goodbye. Now I'm in Zürich. Then I'm in Athens,
following an illuminated escape path to. Where?
I don't want to be Icarus for the duration of this.
Call me Yannis. Call me Dimitris.
Someone shouts 'Let's have it!' Then let us, at last,
have something fucking Hellenic.

For Kitchens

Is the washing machine a clock with an attitude problem?
Is the iron an anchor with acid indigestion?
Is the radio the ghost of my father?
Is the cat my past venom in a panther suit?
Is the rain a million reincarnated dragonflies?
Is my life a trick played on not being dead?
Is that tea ready?

Jorge Luis Borges, Poultry Inspector

'During the 1940s, Borges fell into disfavour with Juan Perón, who removed him as director of the National Library and made him a government inspector of poultry'
   – Perry Higman

You can't hyperlink a chicken   the coop is a special collection grilled with hexagons   You might think texts stay in their place the opposite is fact   Texts crosscheck each other after readers exit while chickens (in fact) have a cogent structure   known to many as the pecking order   Texts mutate new texts   a select few can access them   Chickens recognise a hundred faces   as they bob and weave like boxers in their seventies   colour blindness does not exist in the species   O the world before cataracts!   Texts go into hiding from chief executives   who mismanage their exegesis texts cause them nightmares   While chickens dream in Rapid Eye Movements   in dreams they rule all text   strutting like Shahs through libraries   from London to Tehran   pecking words from each page   Texts are reincarnated battery hens throw a novel from a window & watch the text block flap   they have no paternal instinct for the new   fleecing their sleeves as they sleep   & shrieking like lava creeks   Chickens have over thirty vocalisations   O libraries are coops are clouds are bricks are carnivals   Don't tell Perón this demotion excites my work ethic   counting chickens   makes fiction hatch

When the sun came to speak to me

'This better be good
to make me run like butter over stubble fields,
cutting the corn like the face of a scarecrow
that hasn't been shaved since the day he was stuffed.
The second time I spoke was to Frank, the first Mayakovsky,
if this is another case of third-rate poet with whiner's block,
I'm out. You know, I see more of the world in eight minutes
than you see in a life, even with your "inner world" and "extra vision",
You see
You don't see, with your internalisation & overthink,
if you did, you wouldn't char your thoughts
in the George Foreman grill of your mind, asking for a text
to make you feel alive. Now I've lit your window like an LA dressing room
is that all you can say : 'stress'? Do you think Frank
with his dextrous love-life, & Vlad – with his life on a hook –
didn't feel that too & turn it to its good rich source
of new energy & incendiary creativity?
You've spent your life sending postcards in your head
so you missed the dream flash of the hare beside the lake,
the dunnock in the mulberry bush, the starfield
through your best friend's windscreen. Turn all that weight
to presence, poet. Open the blinds.'

Anschluss

I meet my dead father in the Anschluss.

– What are you doing here dad, you should be dead?
– You can talk, you're supposed to be living in 2022 …

We hug the fierce, fatigued, irritated hug of two people gazumped by death.
I know he's been dead for twenty years, but I've never understood why
I couldn't meet him for a drink.

People are running past us in black clothes and hats, dragging cases & children
by the sleeve. What black hole of history would you not frisk for an hour with
your dead one?

– Dad, should we go for a drink? I've got so much to tell you – I have
   a child now, he's quite grown-up.
– But we can't speak German, how will we order?
– I've learned a bit, we'll be okay.

In a coven of red and gold my dad sits & I order us two pints of Dunkel which
will light up this never-pending afternoon as the world spirals – wirbels –
around us. I place the drinks on the table, making two black lakes that dad
wipes with a mat stating WEIßBIER IST GUD. There's so much to say,
I don't know where to start, but with death's advantage he gets there first :

– What does Anschluss even *mean*?

I sip the Dunkel, thinking.

– Connection.

I say.

How to speak Scouse

Say *I mean* before saying anything.

Repeat everything back to front :
'That was what your dad liked,
your dad liked that.'

Talking nonsense is different from not making sense :
'I wouldn't say you've aged,
you just got older.'

When someone says *tune*, they're not asking you
to hone a wind instrument.
'Tune' announces this song now playing
which demands complete & utter God-given respect.

I mean, when did you last hear music this good?

Then : a ghost

Then : a ghost. A past summer. A distant life.

There : a spectre. A forgotten smile. A hazy field.

That : a ghost ship. Writes its voiles across the seas.

A spectral flashback flares its match-strike.

This : a touch. Ghost claims the skin. Wears our bodies.

A poet & two translators

The translators lose the poet off the coast of Cumbria. He was there one minute & then, like a cancelled saint, gone. 'We had one job there', the first translator says, '& blew it'. 'Hang on', the second says, 'now he's gone we can rewrite his poems for him & translate them how we feel. Let's face it, he wasn't much of a poet, was he?' The storm raises its amp to eleven, spits at a cottage. The translators kick along the shore learning that inspiration is a busy spreadsheet that auto-sums insolvency. 'What have you got?' the first translator asks. The second looks down at a page scratched with glyphs of shorthand and the single word : 'shingle'. 'It's coming along ... & you?' The second translator shows three pages that he later confesses were spat out by AI.

They watch the horizon as a form takes shape. First, what seems to be a seal, which lengthens like an lectern to reveal the poet's head. The poet walks upright through the shallows, seaweed stroking the suede of his jacket. He pulls a cigarette from a pocket, it sags like stem rot & won't light. The translators run to him, like disciples distracted by Black Friday. 'You're back!'/ 'You've re-arrived', they shout in unison. 'Where were you?'

'I wanted to be the first to give voice to the ocean floor but had to learn to hold my breath for six hours. It is dark down there, & light – like adultery on the Sutton Hoo. My throat's dry as a kraken's chuff – what time does Happy Hour run to?'

Talk to that

There came a point
   in human interactions
when people asked
   'Can you talk to that?'
not, 'What are your thoughts?'
  or, 'Can I have your view?'
or even, 'What do you think?'
   but 'Can you talk to that?'
 overnight
the abstract became the object
  a mischief of rhetoric
that removed the person
   from the dialectic.
'Can you talk to that?'
What fractal was detached,
   what was the 'that'
that wanted talking to?
    Heel boy, sit, sit,
get back
talk now, talk to make it sit,
   the question has fleas!
Lice! Tics!
    Can you thought to that?
Can you think that?
  Can you take a that?
Can you talk
 Can
Can you talk to
 Can   can you
Can you talk to that?

Letter to Bez

Bez, post-Victorian Boz, Viz incarnate
and Viceroy of the sinew, what is the name
for light that detracts from the stars?
Urban pollutants de-lux distant galaxies
as we walk after parties through school fields,
via car parks, past vacant vats & waste grounds.
Is the body toxic or is it the body politic
that flexes our muscles for stimulant & toxin?
Bez, flexible wicker man of Manchester,
you would know, your hands in semaphore
over a crowd off their box on whizz & Budvar.
Did you watch Von Trier's *Melancholia*
and dance the planet's Dance of Death
with 'I've got a brand new fridge & a microwave'?
Sun-splashed with lollipops & Haribos,
where did those days go, star-roving
across the umber fortress of the Midland Hotel?
Your thirsty scholars earned major honours
despite lack of internet & mobile phones; landlines,
hearsay
and the March of Converse was all it took
to make a Movement.
O Black Mountain of Didsbury, Beats of Whalley Range,
it was a Grand National of ketamine every Saturday
and now all the horses are dead
who will stop the ringing whinny in each ear?
Spiral-eyed Bez of Oxford Road, is it just me
or does the year try to move to chaff & bran,
chaff & bran, when our pulmonaries are primed
for so much more; SUVs won't always start,
but the passionate of our time dance in more ways
than the maracas of cash can snatch from a moment.
If I start a band tomorrow, would you dance for free
or would a funding grant be necessary?
Would you move sans cash for a flex-wedge of grass?

Governments took such joy
dismantling the gazebo of your visions
and reassembling them as feelgood Britannia,
never to realise that the players exist for the listeners,
but the dancers also dance for the listeners,
dancing only for those that love the music,
making of the good broken chords a kind of tent
pitched in the VIP field of the moment
where all cuts are treated with liquid LSD,
dispensed like droplets to liquefy a cicatrix –
and all of them mere acts for oblivion.
Bez, I overspeak, vexed by your erasure from the textbooks.
Bez Maserati, M. Bezzler, whoreson zed
heard on everyone's tongue but rarely seen in dictionaries,
did you rip across the Heath on a quad bike
as the privileged ripped out their eyes to prove they *felt*?
There are parts of you ripped to shreds of felt
out on that heath, which was drained, then blazed.
The first sign of desperation is getting leery,
then leaking, then taking a group poesis up the wrong tree.
Bez, vex not your ghost, let the old world pass,
dispense kinetic energy like slush down the penny falls,
grind past the arthritic & synthetic until the realist you,
the cackling grocer & underhand dealer,
burst all blackheads into red shift & nova,
and still the body asks : Is the Kronenbourg vegan?
Are the eggs alcoholic? Are the springs in the bunkbeds
made from asparagus? Does anyone eat deep-fried textblocks?
Your dreams turn to green & the days go blue.
Bez, the non-prandial trips to the Czech Republic
are passed, cheeks are pinched & the elastic
is starched at point of party trick.
Is that dust that blows across antique time,
as Coriolanus blistered, or is it the real us
reflected back, at last, without regret?

Our time is this, our colour fuchsia,
our advances left in the green room riders of the Capitol.
Where do the words all go to, sweated & detoxed,
drowned out & forgotten,
all the loves of the endorphin rush spoken
and sent up like pink vowels to heaven.
You talked more 'to the buttock of night than with the forehead
of the morning' & now the buttock talks back –
it's called Opportunism.
Here, take these maracas, take these & show me how one
without a musical sense can be part of something
that helps us live. You shook them & bodies moved,
learned just this one trick, four bars, kept to it,
and we moved sideways to it.
How many times do we go down on our prayer-bones
to make peace with this raft of flesh?
Which Pinkie worked as the cosmic yardstick?
Bez, you made the sun dance in spangle-shapes,
pulled it down into a flashpan with the wheel of a cymbal.
Can it be, after all, that hedonism is the only activism,
that to shut out the daylight hours is to box austerity
like a sloth kept alive in a lead-lined coffin?
Bezman, Bismarck of Salford, Byzantium light of The Haçienda,
it's over & out, except it's not, & never was –
you never died at twenty-eight as the warranty expects,
you went into the marketplace & the comebacks
in rekindled auditoriums musty with Victoriana.
Bez, I'm snowed with nothing burning,
have heard nothing new about your eyes,
I'm delayed ahead of the clearing,
at the door of the darkroom of hedonism
which is to be conscious but not to think
to just be
to be …
the pharmacy is above the brewery,

the app-types in red suits and Justin Bieber t-shirts
walk like they've shit two pounds of tomatoes –
I wouldn't want to be in their shoes.
Have I been presumptuous? Are you staying in this joint?
The drinks aren't cheap, sure, but how palatial
are the walls? First there was God, then was
gossip, then was the almighty godliness
of Erdinger Dunkel.
And Bez, what sounds are to be heard in an ocean
of wax? After so many years cited as a clinger-on
did you make the best of those who clung to you,
faux-friend, acolyte & groupie? Fame creates
a ruse-like force that makes us victims
of its glare, as if to be under its lumens for seconds
transfers its flame into the flue of our house.
Like you, no Sir has come before my name,
only Sir Real, & how you shone like Quint on the Orca,
if only for a moment, then gone.
Like Timon you gave everything away,
but having nothing from the start made it easy
to dig at roots & let the bullion ring the stars.
You were right that to party all night made the day
take care of itself, out in a cave of your own sub-class,
sliding to the centre from the depths of nowhere,
you saw real poverty & wanted to know what life could be,
wrote out your name in BIG FUCKIN CAPITAL LETTTERS
and defined it in self-declared layman's politics
and soapbox orations. You docked your shed
to a ramshackle band that shifted like filtered
Beelzebubs, metamorphosed from gnarled histories
into a radiant oak, your maracas were golden apples,
that swung, were plucked & seem to swing still,
in memory at least, orbed portals to a culture now past,
nights that you filed away like blackouts, like cinema slides,
left out overnight in the Deansgate rain.

Hypnotism

Hypnotism was a Victorian invention for freeing the subconscious.
It made a learning curve from a bending crucifix, eardrums
trademarked as phonographs, discharging wax cylinders.
'Mina, are you there?' the hero asks, with technology in his head,
and the right to read her diary when she faints –
little realising his own is being read by the Professor,
who has The Academy of Demons on his side.

The Lord of Misrule

'When we remember the long array of similar figures, ludicrous yet tragic, who in other ages and other lands, wearing mock crowns and wrapped in sceptred palls, have played their little pranks for a few brief hours or days, then passed before their time to a violent death.'
   – James George Frazer

O Lady of Lourdes pray for me now & in the dour of my earth.
My role : to lead on the drinking of the ale, jeered on by the Exec.
Mere harlequin, merry prankster; a violent death when the ale is drunk.
Take this take on the institution : a squirrel flat at the recycle bin –
the maggot's entrance is the bluebottle's exit. Headstones cluster
in summer & black granite spreads in a grab of clams.
Where are the shores, my Lady? How long must I lead these revelries?
'Keep drinking', our leaders say, so I add some horns to my hat,
ask the Head of Finance to roll with me. 'What a day to not be dead!', I say.
Lady, there are Martian apparitions over your waters, I see them from
        the office window.
You saw your vision while gathering firewood, my only role is to burn it,
with a job description older than the Laureate's, a tongue charred as Polycarp,
but fixed-term contracts lead to a kind of psychosis
when extensions depend on those who have permanence.
Fluids, like your waters, O Lady, are all I have to trade with.
Here come the Exec, with a strategy that came from above,
immaculately conceived through amanuensis, a spasmodic whim.
The office goes dark, a sacred wood in eclipse. We wait for the climax revelation.
'We're out of drink', the Director says. 'Kill him'.

This Thing Happened

We're in the Belvedere & Robert says
'I'm Maximus!' Kirk Douglas de-cubes
into the role of Charles Olson.
Patricia laughs & Sarah says
'Well, that somehow makes sense'.
I go on one about Olson's Gloucester,
pronounced GLOWster, Robert says,
being, I say, the last outpost against
American corporate capitalism.
Robert tells us about
a Kenneth Rexroth poem set in Liverpool
in which the poet visits a prostitute
and she refuses to take the money.
Friendliest city in the world. The thing is,
I've read another Rexroth poem,
set in Oaxaca, where the same thing happens.
Did Rexroth see the spirit animal
of each place in this way
or was he just so good looking?
Last orders has gone, Steve is gathering
the glasses with a lilt in his step
because he's got the next three days off,
and I say : me & Sarah are walking down
to Kavanagh's for a late drink
what say you Patricia & Robert?
But they put a camp peg in the Belv
for a last half there & we walk out
to the long five-minute walk to Kavanagh's,
past the Anglican Cathedral which everyone
knows has its secrets. This is the thing though :
when we walk into Kavanagh's
there's a woman and two men talking

and the woman says: 'What's the name
of that film about the Greek warrior?'
and he says 'Spartacus!' & she says 'Kirk Douglas!'
I order the round under the ceiling's
bazaar of swinging gas masks, Victorian dolls
and a top hat, & I'm thinking how Charles Olson
came to Liverpool once, not everyone knows that.

Hey

Now that you're dead I won't tell you how to live your life
Your oscillation between hedonism & regret
The afterlife begins with no one on your back
Hey, the only one of you there ever was
o
lie
on
When the foxes scratch
Tell them your name

A Biography

When I was new & full of days
and my birth was in darkness
I crawled through heaven's bandwidth
to the sky's thorny outage
placing my cross in the hull
of a timeblind star : I steered,
walking where the graves
were greener, into a headwind
of 'No Shit Shylock'. A globe
rolled over the shyster sand
and the bitten was generous.
I entered corrupt arcades :
sand forts glistered in a cosmos.
I thought it was Florida –
it was Albion forever.
I lay in bed when I cusped
and was hacked by the sun nine times –
a jellyfish veined with lumens.
There was a time my life was trimmed
like the marble rind on a clock
and I watched a moth the size
of a beefsteak climb the glass –
we locked prehensile eyes : it,
with its face like Mozart. That was
the year the meteor landed at
my son's feet, magnetised by fate.
He said, 'it's called SAND because
It is between sea & land'.
They said the sea was a mother
but to me it was a kitten
that had since lost its mother.
I could hear the insides of snails
and sometimes saw with the lens
of a kestrel. Living for this :

the hour when my lungs outspanned
like a jackdaw. God's spirit
was the same as my spirit
so I said twenty-one prayers
and wrote each day, knowing that
Christ was the same as Bacchus.
I believed in a reverse
Paganism in which objects
manifested as Gods. Spirited!
I was played by the weather
like a moodboard & could see
blue in storms & red in snow.
Alcohol made my teenage
anxiety subside; when I
was forty I cut back drink
to reduce my anxiety.
She was my muso, I was hers.
My son became a found poem.
The alphabet lived in the clouds.
Leo-licked & August tanned –
I roared each Summer inside the sun.

Down on the canal on Christmas Day

Down on the canal on Christmas Day
a man walks towards me out of water-light,
upright, Cratchit-wrapped, a smile to say :
I know you. Hello Chris. Ghost in a time-ripped landscape
where a low solstice sun spills whisked
through a metallic staircase.
With joy, the man's smile haunts me for miles –
a long blasted path, where a dead rat's belly festoons
its purple crinoline Christmas hat.

In canal-light, in time-light, in Cratchit-light,
in ripped-light, in rat-light, in Solstice-light,
in metallic-light, in frost-light, in grief-light,
in Christmas-light

from the smile of a stranger
I remake my father.

A poet & two translators

The poet & two translators look at three reports laid out on a desk. 'Today's the day', the poet says, aerating spittle at the mouth, 'when this endless welt of unhappiness pops. What report should we start with?' 'Jung', says the first translator, but the second objects: 'It's got to be Freud. A mind like his', nodding to the poet, 'needs the complete works, chronologically.' The reports are the result of the poet's summer : psychoanalysis each day with Sundays off, known as his deep swim in whiskey's Amber Lake.

The first translator opens the report, the paper crackles like a starched flag. *I have not come across anything like this in my work before, the patient has no superego; his mind is like a zeppelin, long unmoored from a forgotten war and his ego can't land it due to the grimpen mire of his denial.* The poet moves to the open window. 'Farcical', he says, 'who follows Freudian analysis these days anyway? Let's have Jung!' The second translator reads: *I offered the client a range of analytical methods, but his only interest was in sandplay. I left the room for five minutes and came back to find him naked in the pit, telling my assistant to move beyond the symbolic and join him. We won't be seeing him again, please find the bill enclosed.*

The poet has his back turned to the translators, looking out at the street. 'And Lacan?'

The first translator reads: *A fascinating subject, I have never had a patient so openly declare his desire for the Other*. The second translator looks at the page: 'that says *Mother*'. Where the poet was is empty space. The translators close the window to stop the draft coming in.

A walk through the Baltic

A thought is a break
who said that?
as I took cover
learned to jump rope
and move like this morning
the sky suddenly streaked
the Gothic bastard
an ocean liner fused
but over it blue
for the first time in weeks
arriving from Nova Scotia
docking quayside at Seaforth
two dozen fresh loaves
a site workers' break
the sun on my face
of feeling okay
the Keith Haring show
McCarey arrives on land
the best breakfast in days
tomatoes only red
it was three years ago
on a poet's decant
we talk of *Transitional Toys*
then B.V. Thomson
Dreadful Night'
then McCarey's in a cab
to the Baltic Social
when my eyes
and on to Keith Haring
of his practice
then out to the docks
we share on the bench
What wouldn't we have
what would we have left
what rooms unfilled
from this race

in consciousness
The rain in corrugated sheets
from panic
to think 'a thought's just a thought'
quick through the city
in mackerel blue
of the Anglican Cathedral
from bloody thorns
just a taste of blue, but enough
walking to meet McCarey
by cargo boat
then a cab to Baltic Bakehouse
batched & still hot
dipping bread in tea
& a sensation
planning the afternoon
at Tate Liverpool.
an hour before his flight
Colombian coffee
because of the sun
when we met
to Macau
the group exhibition this winter
'The Bastard city of Fucking
as Tom Leonard called it
& I walk through the streets
to meet you, how the room sings
touch your eyes
the colour   the energy   the stamp
dancing through the UV Room
the sap of sea-salt fudge
looking out at the river
if we'd have died at 31
of our selves & our work
what days would be lost
to find happiness?

Notes

'Fathermade, mothermatter' is written after Gail McConnell's 'Untitled / Villanelle' from *Fothermather* (*Ink, Sweat & Tears*, 2019).

'The Machine' is written after W.S. Graham's poetry to his father, during a time of deep immersion in his work when recreating his cottage as a built space in the National Poetry Library. Thanks to David Nowell Smith for the collaboration.

'Scouse' explores the history of the Scouse dialect and accent, which took its name from the Scandinavian dish 'lapskaus' which sailors brought to Liverpool. Scouse came about due to the Irish migration to the city following the Great Famine of 1845-52. By 1851 around 25% of Liverpool's population was Irish-born, spreading the gift of storytelling, poetry and humour through the streets. I love the observation from certain linguists that the nasal, phlegmy aspect of Scouse is down to the people having prolonged colds from the proximity to the Irish Sea and that their children copied them as they spoke, making flu-speak the norm. In 2011 documents emerged which detailed how the Conservative government of the 1980s had considered a policy of 'managed declined' for the city of Liverpool. Rather than treating the social problems of the time, including unemployment, a racist police force and lack of opportunities for the young, geographical amputation was instead seen as an option. 'We fought like the Norse in a fang of redness' is the volta at the midway pivot of this 13-line sonnet, conjuring the Nordic roots and the colours of the Militant council which ran the city.

Threnody of Radiation: *"I swear I can see the sea"* is a quote from the James' song 'Sometimes'.

'Shut Up Michael McClure' is written in response to McClure's performance of his 'animality' poems to a cage of lions in San Francisco Zoo in 1966. This antagonising of these beautiful creatures can be seen on YouTube under 'Michael McClue reading poetry to lions'. My poem offsets this with the incredible poetry of Valzhyna Mort and Laura Tohe who write in the endangered languages of Belarusian and Navajo, respectively.

'When the sun came to speak to me' is written in the tradition of sun conversations made famous by John Donne in 'The Sun Rising'. My poem refers to Frank O'Hara's and Vladimir Mayakovsky's conversations in poetry with the sun. The sun came to speak to me in East Dulwich on 6th February 2025.

'Letter to Bez' is about Happy Monday's dancer Bez. It was written moving between Bez's biography *Freaky Dancin'* and the plays of Shakespeare. Numerous quotes from Shakespeare are embedded in the poem.

'A Walk Through the Baltic' was written while coming through a spell of depression. The first part of the poem describes a walk from Anfield to the Baltic area of Liverpool, passing the Anglican Cathedral which I always think of as 'The Gothic Bastard'. 'McCarey' is the Scottish poet Peter McCarey who sailed from Nova Scotia to Liverpool on a cargo boat where I met him for breakfast. The second half of the poem responds to visiting the Keith Haring exhibition at Tate Liverpool in 2019 with my wife Sarah.

Acknowledgements

Versions of these poems have appeared in the following journals: *Aquifer, Lay of the Land* (zine), *London Magazine, Manhattan Review, Poetry Review*.

Some of the poems were first published in *Talk to That & Other Poems* (pamphlet edition of 50 copies, Tangerine Press, 2020). Thanks to Michael Curran.

A selection of poems appeared in the anthology *Blackwell's Poetry No. 1* edited by A.R. Thompson and MacGillivray.

'The Rambling Boy of Pleasure' was included in *Albion An Island on the Edge of Madness* (New Rivers Press, 2023). Thanks to Robert Montgomery.

A version of 'A Biography' along with 'Ghosts at Sea', 'Been living like this for days', part 1 of 'Threnody of Radiation', 'Meeting Mark Fisher' and 'The Rambling Boy of Pleasure' were included in *Dreamt by Ghosts: Notes on Dreams, Coincidence, & Weird Culture*. Thanks to Dominic Jaeckle.

'For Kitchens' was commissioned by SJ Fowler for *Illuminations VII : Celebrating Friederike Mayröcker*, an event at the Austrian Cultural Forum on 11 September 2019.

Thanks to my editor Jane Commane for having faith in my work and for improving this book through numerous editorial insights.

Thanks to all my friends including Dave, Ed, Isobel, Jon, Pascal, Simon, Tom and Will for conversations, pints and encouragement.

Thanks to my son Pavel – the man who works for passion is always richer than the man who works for money alone.

And always to Sarah, for the first moment of the day to the last at night – and the dreaming between.